25 Things
to **Make** and **Do** in
Adobe® Photoshop®
Elements® 4

Adobe

25 Things to Make and Do in Adobe Photoshop Elements 4

Lisa Matthews

Adobe Press books are published by Peachpit.

Peachpit

1249 Eighth Street
Berkeley, CA 94710
510/524-2178
510/524-2221 (fax)

For the latest on Adobe Press books, go to www.adobepress.com

Find us on the Web at: www.peachpit.com

To report errors, please send a note to errata@peachpit.com

Peachpit is a division of Pearson Education

Copyright © 2006 by Adobe Systems Inc.

Editor: Suzie Nasol
Production Editor: Susan Rimerman
Copyeditor: Liz Welch
Interior design and composition: Danielle Foster
Indexer: Ken Della Penta
Cover design: Mimi Heft

Notice of Rights

Notice of Liability

Trademarks

ISBN 0-321-38481-4

9 8 7 6 5 4 3 2 1

Printed and bound in the United States of America

Contents

Introduction

25 Things to Make and Do with Adobe Photoshop Elements 4 delivers hands-on projects to help you create exciting and professional looking artwork using Photoshop Elements 4.

Working with your own images, logos, and artwork, you will learn how to fix your photos, combine images, and make everything from slide shows, and stationary to fun magnets and tattoos.

Getting organized!

The first project is all about using the Organizer in Photoshop Elements 4 and one that you should definitely not miss.

The Organizer is a powerful database that displays all of your images from folders throughout your system in one Photo Browser. Now you can see all your images from your separate photo files, email attachments, and deeply nested folders in one place. The Photo Browser allows you to scroll through photos and adjust their size from small thumbnails to full size. The Timeline bar above lets you quickly locate photos from a specific month and year.

In the Organizer, you will find Tags and Collections. These are valuable organization tools that work in conjunction with the Organizer's database. Collections lets you pull together files from anywhere on your computer to create groupings like a photo album. Tags let you mark photos and put them into categories and subcategories. Many of the projects in the book use them, so you will want to be familiar with how they work.

Using the projects

Each project has step-by-step instructions and design tips. Some of the projects also include design variations and a choice of templates to help you customize your work.

To get your images ready for any of the projects, follow the instructions in the Quick Fixes project: From there go to the project of your choice. All of the projects contain stand-alone instructions, so just find the project suited to your needs, and get going!

A few of the projects contain templates that you can work with. These templates can be found online at www.peachpit.com/25things. Download the templates as you need them or take them all down and store them on your machine until they're required.

Project 1

Tools:
Photoshop Elements

Materials:
Your photos

Create Custom Photo Catalogs Using the Organizer

Using the Organizer in Photoshop Elements 4.0 for Windows, you can create individual collections and categories of your entire image library.

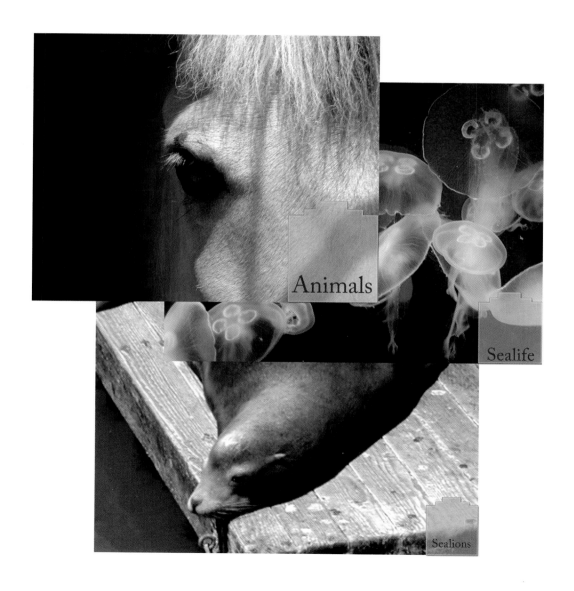

Although it looks like a simple photo-display device, the Organizer is actually a powerful database that lets you see and find images from various drives, folders, and e-mail attachments all in one place. The Organizer allows you to then sort and catalog those images in a variety of ways.

In this project, we create a collection of photos similar to a traditional photo album. This is an easy project that you will probably use often to organize your photos. In the second part of the project, you learn how to categorize your photos using tags. Both collections and tags are fantastic tools for keeping track of all your images, and they allow you to find your images in a snap. They are also essential tools for using creations in Photoshop Elements, such as scrapbooks and slideshows.

Note: The photos you see in the Organizer are not actually stored there, but are still in their original folders. Be careful not to delete photos thinking that the Organizer will save them. If you delete a photo from its original folder, it will be gone and you won't be able to recover it.

Create a Collection in the Organizer

1 **Get started.** If you have not already brought your photos into Photoshop Elements 4, now is the time. Go to the Organizer, and choose File > Get Photos > By Searching. Photoshop Elements will find all the photo files in your computer and open them in the Photo Browser. If you want, you can also bring in images from a variety of other sources, such as CDs, cameras, Flash cards, and even mobile phones by just clicking on the Get Photos button in the menubar.

2 **Create a new collection.** With all your images now in view, you can find those you want to put in your first collection. Select the Collections tab in the right pane of the Organizer. Click New > New Collection. In the Create Collection dialog box, type the subject name and any notes. Then click OK.

3 **Add your photos.** Repeat the process for all the photos you want to put in your collection. To make it easier, pull your images together into a single group and drag them to your new collection. Do this by either pressing the Shift key while selecting (if your images are contiguous) or by pressing the Ctrl key (if they are noncontiguous). Once your images are part of the collection, you will see the Collection icon under it.

Collection icon

4 **Edit the Collection icon.** By default each Collection icon will be the first image in the collection. If you want to use another one, click the Edit Collection(✏). From there, click the Edit Icon button. Use the navigation buttons to select which photo you want, and then crop if desired. Click OK.

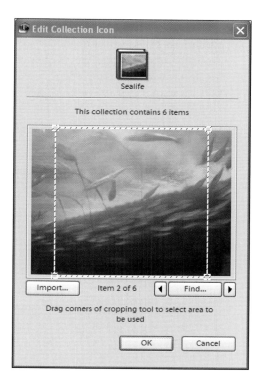

5 Double-click the icon in the Collections pane to view your new collection. That's it!

When you are done, click Back to All Photos to view all your photos.

Create Tags in the Organizer

Tags let you mark photos and put them into categories and subcategories. Inside the Tags pane you'll find preexisting categories of people, places, and things where you can store your finished tags. For example, say you collect animal photos—lots of them. With tags you can tag all of your animal photos "Animals" and make subcategories, such as "Zoo," "Farm," "Forest," "Birds," and "Aquarium." The possibilities are endless.

In this project you tag a set of photos and then create a subcategory.

1 **Create a new tag.** In the Organizer, click on the Tags tab and choose New > New Tag. In the Create Tag dialog box, fill in the name of the subject and any notes you have.

2 **Add your photos.** Follow the same steps as you did when creating your collection. The first image you add will become your icon. Again, if you want edit the icon, follow the same steps as you did with your collection.

3 **Create a subcategory.** First, select the category you want to add to. In the Tags tab, select New > New Sub-Category. In the resulting dialog box, enter a name for your subcategory and click OK. Drag the new icon onto the photos you want to include in your new category.

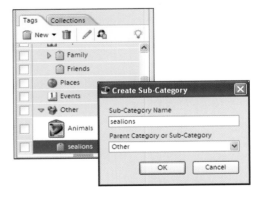

4 **Get organized!** To further organize your photos, you can sort your tags into the icons for favorites, people, friends, places, and events. If you have photos you do not want displayed, tag them with the hidden icon.

Tools:

Photoshop Elements

Materials:

Your photo

Quick Fixes: Get Your Photos Ready for Projects

Learn easy ways to fix such problems as red-eye, incorrect colors, crooked images, and more.

In this first project, you will learn to use some of Photoshop Elements' features to fix common image problems such as red-eye, color casts, and backlighting. Open an image that you'd like to work on and use the techniques that are best suited to your image. Note: Most of the issues mentioned can be dealt with in Quick Fix mode; however, it is a good idea to become familiar with the Standard Edit mode so you can solve more in-depth problems, such as getting rid of blemishes.

Before you start to edit your image, take a look at the following checklist to help ensure a smooth project workflow:

Save a copy of the original image. It's always smart to keep the original version of your photo as a backup in case you need it for any reason. The easiest way to remember to do this is, once you edit your image, just save it with a new name. That way, you can always go back.

Work in RGB mode. In Photoshop Elements, you can work in RGB, Bitmap, Grayscale, or Index color mode. Very rarely will you work in any mode other than RGB. To see what mode your image is in, or to change the mode, choose Image > Mode.

Use the correct image size

Since most projects you will work on—in this book or otherwise—call for a specific dimension, it is important to know how to set the image size.

Whether you are scanning the image yourself, using a digital camera, or simply getting your images from a photo CD, you should know a little about image resolution.

Images in Photoshop Elements are made of pixels. Pixels are small data squares with a specific color value and location.

The resolution of the image refers to the number of pixels per inch (ppi). The rule of thumb is that higher resolution equals higher image quality simply because there is more information. A higher resolution also means a larger file size.

What does this mean for you? First, to check the resolution of your image, choose Image > Resize > Image Size.

Notice that the dialog box that appears has two different sections. One gives you the actual pixel dimensions—the size the image will appear on screen—and the other gives you the document size—the resolution and print dimensions plus the file size.

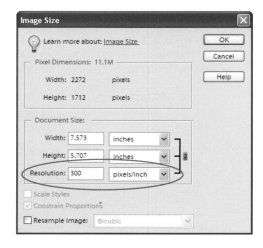

Set the resolution

You can change the resolution and print dimensions of the image by entering a higher or lower value. When you do this and the Resample Image box is checked, Photoshop Elements will either add pixels (sample up) or throw them away (downsample). Another rule of thumb: Never sample your images up. Doing so will result in poor image quality as Photoshop Elements can only estimate what information to add; however, downsampling to make your image smaller is generally fine. Ideally, use an image with the resolution and size closest to what is needed for the final output. To get an idea of what resolutions to use, look at the following examples.

A 72-ppi image (left) resampled up to 150 ppi (right) results in poor image quality.

A 300-ppi image (left) downsampled to 150 ppi (right) results in adequate image quality.

200 to 250 ppi—For most professional offset presses; used for color magazines and brochures.

**16K file size
72 x 108 pixel dim.
1"x 1.5" print size
72-ppi resolution.**

**176K file size
200 x 300 pixel dim.
1" x 1.5" print size
200-ppi resolution.**

72 ppi—For screen viewing of Web pages or online materials.

120 to 150 ppi—For output to typical desktop laser and inkjet printers.

Crop and straighten your photo

Look at your image. Is it straight? Do you want to use the whole image or just a section? There are several ways to crop and straighten your image. The one you choose will depend on how much you want to crop.

Trim and straighten your photo. If your image is crooked because of a sloppy scan, the easiest way to fix it is to choose Image > Rotate > Straighten and Crop Image. Elements will automatically crop and straighten it for you.

Perhaps your image is crooked because of a bad camera angle, or maybe you just want to get rid of an insignificant element in the outer corner. Select the Crop tool ( ) from the toolbox. Then click and drag around the area of the image that you want to keep. Once the area is selected, you can perform any of the following actions:

• Drag a corner or edge to resize the area of the crop.

• Place the cursor over a corner handle and drag in the direction you want to rotate.

• Place the cursor inside the bounding box and drag to reposition it.

When trying to straighten your image, find a true 90-degree angle to use to align your Crop tool. Pillars and picture frames work well, for example.

When you have finished, press Enter to complete the crop. If you change your mind, press Esc to cancel.

Variation: Crop to an exact dimension and resolution

You may occasionally need to crop to an exact dimension and resolution. For example, you may need a headshot that is 1 inch by 1 inch and 150 dpi. To achieve this, select the Crop tool. Notice that the options bar now gives you a place to enter height, width, and resolution. Enter your values. Now when you drag the Crop tool, it will allow only those dimensions.

Make sure that the image resolution is higher than or equal to the one to which you are cropping to avoid sampling up.

Red Eye Removal tool

The common problem of red-eye is now easily fixed using the Red Eye Removal tool ( ). In either Quick Fix or Standard Editor you can quickly and easily change eyes back to their correct color. Note: When you import images to the Organizer you also have the option of letting Photoshop Elements automatically fix any red-eye that it detects.

1 **Zoom in.** It's always a good idea to zoom in on the area you want to edit so you can see the details. Choose the Zoom tool ( ) from the toolbox. Click on the area of the red eye until you can easily work with it.

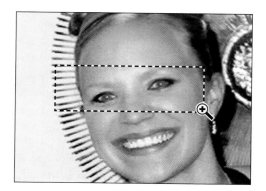

2 **Remove the red.** Select the Red Eye Removal tool ( ) and then click on the red-eye area. The red-eye problem will be fixed once you release the mouse!

Healing Brush tool

The Healing Brush allows you to get rid of minor dermal imperfections from your photo subjects by sampling a good area and then applying that sample to the bad area. The Healing Brush feature ( ) is split into two parts: the Spot Healing Brush tool (commonly referred to as the "zit zapper") and the Healing Brush tool. The former is for small spots and the latter for larger areas.

1 **Select your brush.** To use either function, click and hold on the arrow in the corner of the Healing Brush icon in the toolbar and choose the desired option. In the options bar choose the size and type of brush you need.

2 **Spot be gone!** For the Spot Healing Brush, simply click on the spot you want to remove and poof! The spot is gone! For the Healing Brush tool, Alt-click on an area of the image that you want to sample. Then click on the area you want to cover up. If it is a larger area (a Band-Aid for example), you may need to click a few times to cover the whole area.

Correct the lighting

Correct for uneven lighting. You may take a picture where the lighting is harsh or uneven. The subject could be in front of a window, a sunset, or some other light source. One way to avoid this problem is to use an on-camera flash. Even so, some of your photos will have lighting problems. Fortunately, Photoshop Elements provides a feature that easily remedies the problem.

In Quick Fix mode you can easily adjust the lighting by using the sliders under Lighting. To correct lighting problems in Standard Edit mode, choose Enhance > Adjust Lighting > Shadows/Highlights. Make sure that the Preview box is checked; then use the sliders to adjust the shadows, highlights, and contrast until you are satisfied with the results.

Enhance your colors

Sometimes your photo may have an unnatural color tint. Fluorescent lighting, tungsten lights, and bad scans are just a few of the potential culprits. There are a few ways to fix this in Photoshop Elements 4.0.

Correct color casts. In Quick Fix mode you can use the sliders under Color to remove color problems or just click the Auto button. For a little more control you can use the Standard Edit mode. Select Enhance > Adjust Color > Remove Color Cast. Move your cursor into the image area and click on an area that is supposed to be gray, white, or black. Under the same menu, select Adjust Color for Skin Tone. Use the eyedropper tool to sample a skin tone, and Photoshop Elements will then adjust the colors of the entire photo to that sample.

Sharpen the photo

Many photos can use a little sharpening. The Unsharp Mask filter works great to sharpen image details. If you have adjusted the resolution of your image, it is best to make this the final step of your photo correction.

Set the zoom percentage to 100%. Double-click the Zoom tool (⊕) to set the photo to 100% magnification.

Sharpen the image. Choose Filter > Sharpen > Unsharp Mask. Select the Amount slider and drag until you see a positive result. To preview a specific part of the image, place the cursor in the regular image and move it to the specific area of interest (the cursor will turn into a box). You might want to look closely at hair, eyes, and foliage, where sharpening can be dramatic. It's easy to apply this tool to fix blurry pictures, but over-sharpening can also leave your image with a distracting grainy texture.

Save the file

When you are happy with the final results of your image, choose File > Save As, rename the file, and save it in Photoshop format (.psd).

Project 3

Create Picture Packages

Duplicate your image in multiple sizes for print.

Have you ever had an image that you wanted to make into a holiday card or duplicate for friends and relatives? Here is a quick and easy way to create a multiple-picture layout using just one file.

1 **Edit your image.** In either the Quick Fix or Standard Edit mode, make all of the necessary edits to the image you want to use. Since you will be printing it, the resolution should be between 150 dpi and 300 dpi, depending on how big you want the prints to be. Save a copy of the file. You can also leave the file open if you want.

2 **Choose your file**. Choose File > Print Multiple Photos. This will bring up the Print Photos window, with your photo in the left-hand pane.

3 **Set layout options.** Under Select Type of Print, choose Picture Package. Under Select a Layout, choose a template that will suit your options. Finally, click the Fill Page With First Photo check box.

4 **Go.** Click OK to create your picture package. When it is done, save the file. Your image is now ready to print!

Variation: Print Multiple Images

Sometimes, you may have a number of prints from an event that you want to print. Obviously, you don't want to waste paper or time. This feature allows you to lay out multiple images on one page.

Select your images. In the Organizer, hold down the Ctrl key and choose your images. (This allows you to select non-contiguous images.) Then follow steps 2 and 3 from before, but this time, do not select the Fill Page With First Photo check box. The images that you selected will now be used in the multiple layout.

Project 4

Tools:

Photoshop Elements

Materials:

Your photos

Create a Panoramic Image

Let Photoshop Elements automatically create your panoramic image, or do it yourself.

This technique is for all those fabulous scenes where your camera lens isn't quite wide enough or you are looking for a spanning vista that just isn't possible in one photo. This method is also useful for piecing together building facades. In any event, it's easy to use and fun.

① **Organize your images.** Once you have all the images you want to combine, place them in one folder for easy access.

② **Choose your files.** In the Organizer window, hold down the Ctrl key; this allows you to select noncontiguous images. Then, select File > New > Photomerge Panorama. In the resulting dialog box, your files will appear in the Photomerge Source Files window. Click OK to bring them into the Photomerge window.

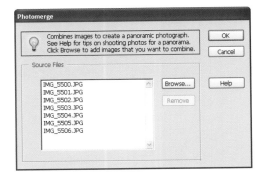

③ **Merge your images automatically.** After you have selected all your files, click OK. Photoshop Elements will then begin to auto-match your images together. When it has finished, you should see the merged images in the Photomerge dialog box, as in the example above.

④ **Merge your images manually.** Photoshop Elements may not always be able to place all your images automatically. When this happens, it will place your images in the thumbnail box above the arranging area. To manually arrange your images, choose the Select Image tool (↖) from the toolbox and then drag the thumbnail into the arranging area.

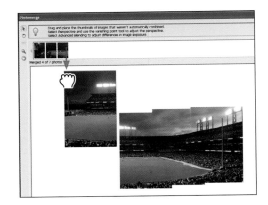

5 **Set up your options.** When your image is selected in the arranging area, you will see a red highlight around it. The dialog box at the right contains all the options for merging your images.

To get things started, you may want to turn on Snap to Image. Next, click Perspective to set the vanishing point. Select the Vanishing Point tool from the toolbox, and click the image where the vanishing point should be. You will see the images adjust to that perspective. Note: Depending on how your images were shot, you may want to use the Rotate Image tool as well.

Finally, to eliminate any differences in exposure, choose Advanced Blending and click Preview. You may still need to do some touch-up in the final file. If you are happy with the result, click OK. Elements will then create a new untitled file with your combined image.

6 **Edit your new file.** Okay, you have your new panoramic image, but it still looks a little less than perfect. Use the Crop tool ( ) to edit out the ragged edges, and make any other edits the image may need, such as adjustments to the color, lighting, and other properties. Choose File > Save As and save your panoramic image with a new name.

Variation: Merging other images

The Photomerge feature doesn't have to be used to create horizontal panoramas. For instance, on your trip through Italy, you may find all sorts of grand church façades, but suppose your camera lens isn't wide enough to capture them? Shoot each part of the façade and then piece the view back together using Photomerge.

You may be wondering if there are any good tricks for creating a panorama or other type of merged image. Take a look at the examples here for some tips on how to create seamless, natural-looking merged imagery.

RULE OF THIRDS It's best if your images can overlap by a third (or more). This gives you something to match up.

EXPOSURE Keep the exposure as consistent as possible. This will help you avoid spending time performing lighting and color edits while making a seamless panorama.

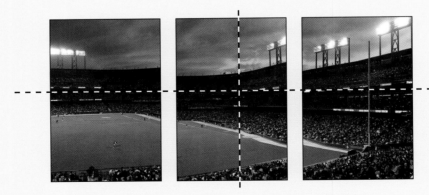

DON'T MOVE! Seriously, when you are shooting images that you plan to merge, stay in the same place. This is an instance where you want to, at the very least, keep the same height and perspective. Some cameras have features that help with this. If creating panoramas is your thing, this is something to look for. Just remember: The more angle changes you make, the more finessing you'll need to do with the Perspective tool.

Project 5

Tools:
Photoshop Elements

Materials:
Your photo

Swap and Add Colors in Your Photographs

Use the painting tools in Photoshop Elements to change or add colors in your photographs.

In this project, you'll learn two different techniques. Working with the Paintbrush tools, you'll learn how to add colors to black-and-white images; then we'll show you how to replace existing colors in images with completely new ones.

In the first technique, we'll demonstrate how to add colors to either a color or a black-and-white image. You can use this method to colorize old photos or to just have fun with new ones!

1 **Get started.** Open your image in Photoshop Elements in the Standard Edit mode.

2 **Remove the current colors.** Unless the image you are using is already a black-and-white image, you will want to remove the colors. To do so, choose Enhance > Adjust Color > Remove Color.

Note: If you are working on a black-and-white image, you'll need to change the image mode to one that allows colors. Choose Image > Mode > RGB Color. This allows you to colorize the image.

3 **Create a new layer.** If the Layers palette is not open, click the Layers arrow to open it or choose Window > Layers. Click the New Layer button (⬛) at the top of the palette.

4 **Set layer options.** You should always give your layers a descriptive name. This way, even if your file has 50 layers, you can easily identify the one you want. Double-click in the Name field inside the new layer and type *colors* as the layer name.

Next, you will set the layer blending mode. The blending modes are located on the pop-up menu next to the opacity settings on the Layers palette. Click the menu and select Color. This setting allows the image to show through the color.

6 **Choose your paint color.** At the bottom of the toolbox, click the Set Foreground Color swatch. Click in the square box to open the Color Picker. Use the vertical sliders to find the color area you desire. Then, use the circle to select the exact color you want. Alternatively, choose Window > Color Swatches and click the color you want. You should see the color you've selected in the square in the upper right of the Color Picker box.

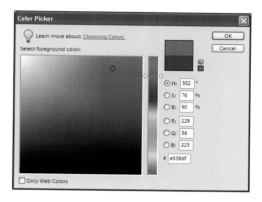

5 **Pick your paintbrush.** Select the Paintbrush tool ( ) from the toolbox. From the Brushes pop-up menu on the options bar, select a medium-size brush for painting. The brush settings appear on the options bar after you select a brush. Note: The brush size also depends on the resolution of your image. A medium-sized brush for a 300-dpi image will be a large brush for a 72-dpi image.

7 **Begin painting.** Select your new layer and zoom in on the area you want to paint. Drag your paintbrush over the area to apply the new color. If you find that your brush is too large, too small, or wrong in some other way, go back to the Brushes menu and select a new brush.

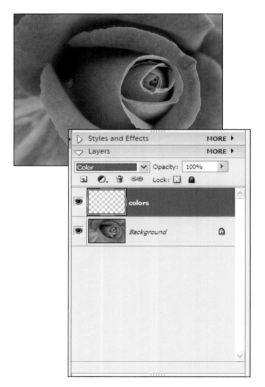

8 **Make corrections.** It happens to the best of us: we make a mistake or change our minds. There are three ways to deal with this. If you just applied the action, press Ctrl+Z. If you want to undo more than one step, go to the Undo History palette. This nifty palette allows you to go back up to 20 steps! The final option for correcting a mistake is to use the Eraser tool ( ). This tool has three forms: Eraser, Background Eraser, and Magic Eraser. Here, just choose the plain Eraser tool. After you have chosen the eraser mode, you can choose Brush, Pencil, or Block. Specify a setting that complements your current paintbrush and drag over the appropriate area.

9 **Experiment with color.** To add more colors, just go back to step 6 and choose a new color.

Create new layers for your new colors and experiment with different layer modes and paintbrushes.

Save a working version. To save your new version with layers, choose File > Save As, rename the file, and save the file in Photoshop format. If you want to save a single-layer (flattened) version, choose File > Save As, rename the file, and deselect the Layers check box. The Save a Copy check box will automatically be selected. Rename your file and save it.

Variation: Replace existing image colors with completely new ones

Open your photo.

Set up your brush tool. Choose the Color Replacement tool ( ), and set Limits to Contiguous. Then specify 50% to 60% for the Tolerance setting. Leave the Mode set to Color.

Sample color to replace. Zoom in and Alt+click on the color you want to replace.

Choose your color and paint! Use a fairly large soft brush for areas with obvious borders. For areas with a less obvious border or a broader color spectrum, go back and set a lower tolerance.

Experiment!

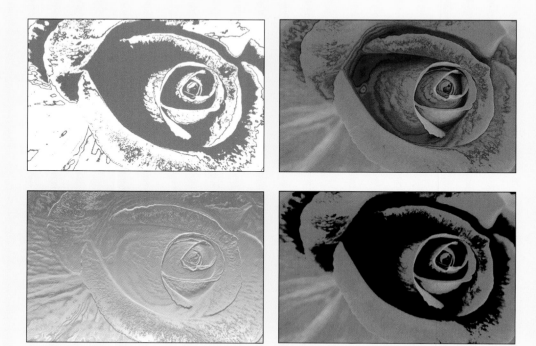

CREATE YOUR OWN LOOK! Try out different filters under Styles and Effects, such as Stamp, to create a whole new look.

HIGHLIGHTS Create a highlight by hand-painting one object in your image.

Project 6

Tools:

Photoshop Elements

Materials:

Your photo

Make Your Subject Pop Out

Put your subject in a whole new setting by manipulating the background or changing it altogether.

A fun and easy way to make sure that your subject is the focal point of your photo is to use Photoshop Elements' Selection Brush (✐). This tool allows you to select and separate your subject from the background so you can edit it or change it completely.

① **Get started.** Open the image you want to edit in Photoshop Elements.

② **Zoom in on your subject.** Using the Zoom (⊕), click an edge of the foreground subject.

③ **Set your masking options.** Using the Selection Brush tool, create your selections by painting the area you want to select either in Selection mode or Mask mode. In Mask mode, the Selection Brush tool selects the inverse of what you are selecting while giving you a colored preview of the mask you are creating over your subject.

Once you have zoomed in on your subject, select the Selection Brush (✐), which is located under the Magic Selection Brush tool. On the options bar, select the Mask mode. Set the opacity to 50%. You can also change the mask color or leave it set to the default red.

This will allow you to see the selection mask you are creating over your subject more clearly.

④ **Choose your brush.** Now that you have set your mask options, you want to do the same for your brush.

Click the Brushes pop-up menu. As you can see by scrolling through the list, there are many options. Start with a medium-sized soft brush. The size will depend on the resolution of your image. The higher the resolution, the smaller the brush will appear; the lower the resolution, the larger the brush will appear.

⑤ **Select your edges.** To make your life easier, first set the edge boundaries and then move inward. Start by painting around the edges of your subject. We are using a soft brush to avoid the harsh cutout look. A softer selection around your subject allows you to blend your final background in a more natural fashion. If you accidentally paint where you don't want to, switch to Selection mode on the options bar and paint over the area. Or you can hold down the Alt key and paint back over; this will subtract from your selection.

6 **Complete the mask.** Once you've finished selecting the edge of your subject, select a larger, hard-edged brush from the Brushes menu. Paint freely inside your new edge until your subject is covered.

7 **Select your subject.** Toggle back to the Selection mode. You should see the selection marquee around your subject and background edges. The background area around your subject is now selected. To isolate your subject within its own selection, choose Select > Inverse. This reverses your selection.

8 **Create a new layer.** Choose Layer > New > Layer Via Copy. This will place a copy of just your subject on a new layer. The Layers palette shows two separate layers: one for the background and another above it that should contain a copy of your subject.

9 **Alter the background.** On the Layers palette, click the Background layer to select it. Choose Filter > Blur > Gaussian Blur. Drag the slider until you get an effect you are happy with. Because you have selected only the Background layer, your subject will not be affected. If you are not satisfied with the results, or if you want to try another filter, choose Edit > Step Backward, press Ctrl+Z, or use the back arrow ( ).

10 **Save a working version of your photograph.** It's always smart to save a layered working version of your file in case you want to make changes down the road. To save your new version with layers, choose File > Save As, rename the file, and save it in Photoshop format (.psd). If you want to save a single-layer version (commonly known as a flattened version), choose File > Save As, rename the file, and deselect the Layers check box. The Save a Copy check box will automatically be selected. Rename your file and save it.

Variation: Experiment with filters

Photoshop Elements has lots of filters and interesting effects. Now that you have your background on a separate layer, you can experiment with filters. Expand the Styles and Effects palette and choose Filters from the Select a Category pop-up. Select All from the Select a Library pop-up. When you see a filter you want to try, select it and click Apply.

Background Cuttout filter

Background with Clouds filter

Variation: Adjust the color of the background

Sometimes it can really be effective to change or remove the color of the background. To do this, choose Image > Enhance > Adjust Color. Then you can choose Hue/Saturation, Replace Color, Remove Color, or Color Variations.

Variation: Use a different image for the background

By now, you are probably realizing that your choices are fairly limitless. You may even be wondering how to go about placing your subject on a whole new background.

1 **Add a new background image.** Open the photo or image that will be used for the new background. (Make sure that your working file is still open and that the Background layer is selected.) Place the two image windows side by side. With your new image active, select the Move (⬆️) from the toolbox. Click the image and drag the new background into your original working file. Note: If the photo bin is open, you may have to either close it or choose Window > Cascade in order to see the two files side by side.

2 **Position the new background.** Select your working file. On the Layers palette, select your new background layer. Use the Move tool to move it to a position that works with your subject. Save your file.

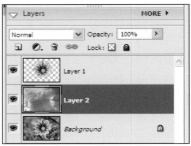

Photoshop Elements' Selection Brush Mask mode allows you to easily select odd-shaped areas in your image. If you are in Mask mode, a temporary colored overlay appears over the unselected areas and exposes the selected areas of the image. When you toggle back to Selection mode, you will see the "marching ants" marquee around the selection you made.

Selected areas

Masked area

Painting with the Selection Brush in Mask mode gives you a colored preview of the area you are masking out.

When you toggle back to Selection mode, you will see the resulting selection.

Tools:

Photoshop Elements

Materials:

Border templates
Your photo

Accent Your Photograph with a Border

Add a finishing touch to your image by using a border.

Placing a border around your photograph is one of the best ways to add a finishing touch. Using the Cookie Cutter tool in Photoshop Elements is a great and easy way to accomplish this. In this project you will learn how to apply premade frames using the Cookie Cutter tool and how to use the Cookie Cutter crop shapes to make unique frames.

1 **Get started.** Open the photograph or image you want to use in Photoshop Elements.

2 **Create new adjustment layer.** Click the Adjustment Layer icon (⬤) located at the top of the Layers palette. Choose Solid Color from the pop-up menu. You will use this new layer to create your border.

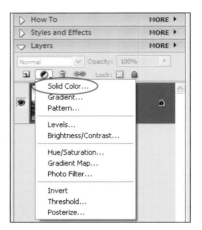

3 **Choose a Color for the border.** Pick a color in the Color Picker dialog box and click OK. (Since this is an adjustment layer you can change the color at any time by double-clicking the color swatch in the layer). Your new layer will completely cover your photo until you apply the frame in the next step.

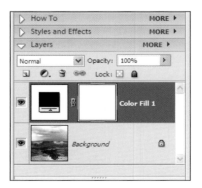

4 **Select your border.** Select the Cookie Cutter tool (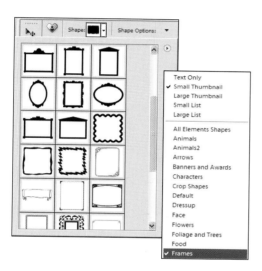) and click Shape on the options bar. In the Shape pop-up palette, click the arrow to view all the available shapes. Select Frames. To better view the frames, change to Large Thumbnail view. When you find a frame you like, double-click to select it, and then close the window.

5 **Frame it!** Click in the upper-left corner and drag to the lower-left corner to frame your whole photo. Adjust the size however you want. When you are done, press Enter to apply the frame.

Variation: Create unique borders using the Cookie Cutter crop shapes

If you are looking for some less conventional borders, try using the crop shapes instead of frames.

1 **Make a copy of your photo.** Open the photo that you want to frame. On the Layers palette, click the Background layer and drag it over the New Layer icon. This will create a copy of your photo. It's important to make a copy, in case you want to change your photo later on.

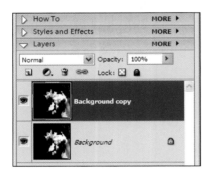

2 **Make a new Background layer.** Select your original Background layer, and follow steps 2 and 3 from the previous instructions to create a new Background layer. This will become the background after you crop your photo.

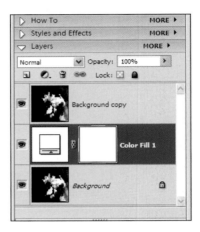

3 **Select your shape.** Select the Cookie Cutter tool and click Shape on the options bar. In the Shape pop-up palette, click the arrow to view all the available shapes. Select Crop Shapes. To better view the crop shapes, change to the Large Thumbnail view. When you find a shape you like, double-click to select it, and then close the window.

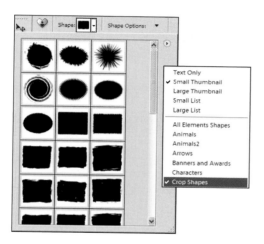

4 **Crop it!** Click in the upper-left corner and drag to the lower-left corner to frame your whole photo. Adjust the size however you want. When you are done, press Enter to apply the crop.

A little border can go a long way. Try to avoid borders that are so overly colorful, large, or complex that they overtake the photograph. Here are a couple of tips to keep in mind when creating borders.

When you create your border, remember that the attention is supposed to be on the image, not the border. Make sure that the size and colors are appropriate for the image.

If you will be placing the photo in a publication, you don't need to add a keyline around the photo. Your image has a stylized border already, so you won't want another one.

STYLES

Choose a border style that matches your subject matter. For example, ornate borders can often be used with images of historical or traditional content, while a contemporary border can work with an offbeat image.

Project 8

Tools:

Photoshop Elements
InDesign (Optional)

Materials:

Newsletter template
Your photos

Publish Your Photographs in a Newsletter

Get your color photos ready for black-and-white or one-color reproduction.

Let's say you're putting together a short newsletter for work, school, or a holiday family update. More than likely, it will be printed in black and white. This project gives you the steps to get your image ready.

When you are done editing your image, you can place it in the page layout program of your choice. We've included a newsletter template that you can use if you have a copy of Adobe InDesign CS, but it's not required for this project.

1 **Get started.** You should decide what photos you want to use and what the final printed size will be. Check the resolution of your images. The resolution should be at least 150-300 pixels per inch.

2 **Open your photo.** Open your first photograph in Photoshop Elements. Take a hard look at it. Are there distractions that could be taken out? Do you want to zoom in on just one person?

3 **Trim and size the image.** Select the Crop (⌷) to trim your image to the correct dimensions. Use the options bar to set the exact image size. If the entire image needs to be smaller, choose Image > Resize > Image size and enter the dimensions.

If you are going to use the optional InDesign template, use the following image dimensions for the front page: 2.65 inches wide by 2.65 inches high for the first image, and 1.69 inches wide by 1.69 inches high for the second image.

4 **Remove the color.** To convert your image to grayscale, choose Image > Mode > Grayscale and click OK. (Remember that it's always a good idea to save a backup version in color before converting your image.)

5 **Adjust the contrast and sharpen.** You may notice a loss of contrast and tonal range when converting from color to grayscale. If this is the case, choose Enhance > Adjust Lighting Levels. Drag the triangular sliders under Input Levels to adjust the tonal range. Make sure the Preview box is checked so you can see what is happening to your image. (For more information on levels, refer to online help.)

Finally, to make your image a little snappier, choose Filter > Sharpen > Unsharp Mask. Drag the Amount slider until you are satisfied with the result. Remember to look at detailed areas such as hair, eyes, and foliage. These areas will often benefit from sharpening. Also keep in mind that too much sharpening is not good for smooth areas such as skin tones or blue skies, which tend to become grainy.

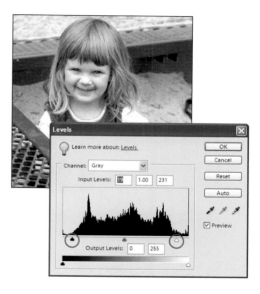

6 **Save in TIFF format.** One of the widely used printing formats is TIFF. To save your document as a TIFF file, choose File > Save As and save your changes in TIFF format. Make sure you also save the original version.

You are now ready to place your image in InDesign or any other layout software. On the companion site, grab P08_tmp.t8 from the Project 8 folder to your hard drive, then open in InDesign.

Variation: Add a little color

Here is a great technique if you are printing on a personal color printer and want an image with a certain hue: for example, if you are going to print a head shot, and you want it to have a warm sepia tone.

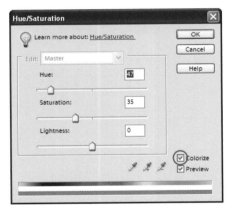

Note: If you are using a professional printer and want to add a color, the image will be called a duotone, and the printer will set it up for you.

1 **Remove the color.** In this process, your image will stay in RGB mode; however, you still need to remove the color. To do this, choose Enhance > Adjust Color > Remove Color.

2 **Add back one color.** In this next step, you will be working with an adjustment layer. Adjustment layers provide a marvelous way to apply edits to your image that are nondestructive—which means that you can go back and change the edits at any time.

Click the Layers arrow to open the Layers palette. Click the Adjustment Layers (⬤) located at the top of the palette. Choose Hue/Saturation.

3 **Adjust the hue.** First, make sure the Colorize box is checked. Then drag the Hue slider until you see your desired color. Experiment with the saturation of the color by dragging the Saturation slider. When you are satisfied with the result, click OK. If you want to change the settings later, double-click the layer thumbnail on the Layers palette.

4 **Save an export version.** Again, save the original; then choose File > Save As, rename the file, and save the file in TIFF format.

When using a page layout program such as InDesign, you can choose an accent color for text, graphics, and images. If you go to a print shop, this will be called a spot color. This process is most commonly referred to as printing a duotone. In choosing your spot color, you should select a color that will work in a variety of tint percentages or shades. Here are some good tips for working with color.

100%	■ type	■ type	■ type
85%	■ type	■ type	■ type
70%	■ type	■ type	■ type
55%	■ type	■ type	■ type
40%	■ type	■ type	■ type
25%	■ type	■ type	■ type
10%	■ type	■ type	■ type

WORKS FOR EVERYTHING
Your color needs to be dark enough to be used for type as well as for photos.

100%	■ type	■ type	■ type
85%	■ type	■ type	■ type
70%	■ type	■ type	■ type
55%	■ type	■ type	■ type
40%	■ type	■ type	■ type
25%	■ type	■ type	■ type
10%	■ type	■ type	■ type

BEWARE Light colors such as yellow, orange, and cyan can disappear at tints of less than 80 percent.

Project 9

Create Calendars Using the Creation Feature

Let Photoshop Elements' Creation feature automatically create a calendar using your own images.

January 2005

In this project you will learn how to create a calendar using the Creation feature in Photoshop Elements.

① **Get started.** To begin, you'll create a collection with 12 images (to represent the months). In the Organizer's Collections tab, click New and select the images from the Photo Browser for your new collection. Save your new collection with the title for your scrapbook.

Note: If you need help with making a new collection, see Project 1.

② **Choose and set up your creation.** Double-click your new collection icon so that you are viewing only those images. Next, click the Create icon ( ). The images in your collection will automatically be selected for your scrapbook.

In the Creation Setup dialog box, choose Calendar Pages and click OK. Step 1 is the Creation Set-up. Choose the style of calendar you want and set your other options such as captions, and title page. Click Next step when you are done.

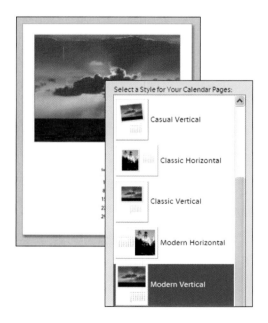

3 **Arrange your photos.** In the next dialog box, you will see all of your images in the order that they will appear on your calendar. To change the order, simply click on the image and drag it the position you want.

4 **Add your captions.** In the Customize dialog box, add the title of your scrapbook by double-clicking in the box below the title photo. Use the arrow keys on the side of the image to add the next caption. If you don't want the caption, click on the caption box and press delete. Click Next Step to save your creation.

5 **Create!** In the Save dialog box, give your creation a name and click Save. Decide how you want to distribute your calendar: you can create a PDF, or print it to your home printer. Then click Done.

Variation: Use the Editor to customize your calendar

Add some fun! Use the Photoshop Elements Editor to add borders, filters, or whatever you want to images destined for your calendar.

Project 10

Tools:
Photoshop Elements

Materials:
Your photos

Create Albums Using the Creation Feature

Use Photoshop Elements to create an album of special memories.

Have you ever wanted to create a card or an album as a gift or for a special occasion? The Creation feature in Photoshop Elements lets you do this quickly and easily using your digital images.

This project shows you how to create a album quickly and easily.

1 **Get started.** To begin, create a collection with the images you want to include in your album. In the Organizer's Collections tab, click New and select the desired images from the Photo Browser. Save your new collection using the title for your album.

Note: If you need help with creating a new collection, see Project 1.

2 **Choose your creation.** Double-click your new collection icon so that you are viewing only those images. Then, click the Create icon ( ), and the images in your collection will be selected for your album automatically.

In the Creation Setup dialog box, choose Album Pages and click OK. In Step 1 of the Create Photo Album Page dialog box, choose the style of photo album and specify how many photos you want per page.

3 **Arrange your photos.** Once you can see all of your photos in the Arrange window, simply click and drag them to where you want. The photos will automatically be re-sorted.

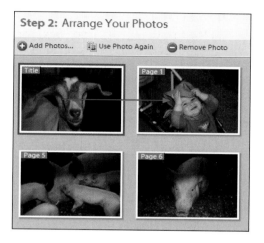

4 **Add your captions.** In the Customize dialog box, double-click in the box below the title photo to add the title of your album. Use the arrow keys on the side of the image to add the next caption. If you don't want any caption, simply click the caption box and press Delete. Then click Next Step to save your creation.

5 **Create!** In the Save dialog box, type a name for your creation and click Save. At this point, specify how you want to distribute your new album: create a PDF, print it, e-mail it, or post it to an online gallery. Then click Done.

Variation: Use the Editor to customize your album

Add some fun! Use the Photoshop Elements Editor to add borders, filters, or whatever you want to images destined for your scrapbook.

Project 11

Tools:

Photoshop Elements

Materials:

Text of your recipe
Photo of final dish

Create a Recipe Book

Now you can publish your own custom recipe book for friends and family.

Salmon with Feta and Spinach

5 Salmon Steaks
1 lb of spinach
1/2 lb of feta

Mix spinach and feta into dry paste. Stuff Salmon steaks and grill for 15 minutes or less.

Notes: Wines that go really good with dish are spicy zinfandels with a good bouquet.

Are you a home chef? The person every-one calls when they need to know what they can substitute for eggs? It's time to put all those masterpieces into a book! This project will walk you through doing just that. All you need are your recipes and the photos that you want to accompany them. First you will size and edit your photos in the Editor, and then move over to the Organizer to create the final book.

1 **Size and edit your photos.** Open Photoshop Elements, and in the Welcome window choose Edit and Enhance Photos. Open the photos that you plan to use for your recipes and resize them so that they are approximately 4x6 inches. The resolution should be at least 150 to 300 dpi for the best quality. Make any additional edits, such as lighting or color correction.

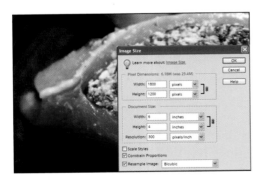

2 **Save!** Save as a .psd file with your layers in case you want to make any changes later. Make sure the Include in Organizer check box is selected. (It is selected by default.) This is your first page! Once you have done this for all of your photos, it's time to move over to the Organizer.

3 **Create a collection.** In the Organizer, click the new Collection icon (▣). Select New Collection, and then type a name. Once you've created your collection, select all of the photo files for your reci-pes and drag them to the new collection. Double-click the collection to view only these photos.

4 **Select your book style.** Now that you have your collection open, click the Cre-ate icon (▦). Choose Album Page and select a style. Some of the styles that work well for this project are Simple; Casual and Classic and Decorative; and Formal and Scrapbook.

Alternately, you can select Bound Book if you want to have your recipe book printed by an outside source.

5 **Add your recipe text.** Once you have selected the style for your book, click Next Step. At this point, you can decide if you want to include a title page and how many photos you want per page. In this case, specify one photo per page. Click Next Step.

Double-click the caption, and enter the recipe text that goes with each photo. If you have text file for your recipes, you can copy and paste it into the text window. Once you've entered the text in the window, you can change its font, size, and color. Click Done when you have finished. Notice that you can move the text around the page for the best placement. If you want to add more text, such as a title or cooking notes, click the Add Text button. Use the navigation arrows to move to the next photo.

6 **Save your book!** When you have finished adding all of your recipes, click Next Step to save your project. Now you can create a PDF, print it straight to your printer, or even e-mail it to a friend. Note: If you are planning on having your recipe book printed elsewhere, choose PDF to create one final book file. That's it!

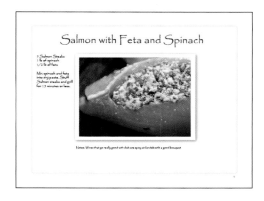

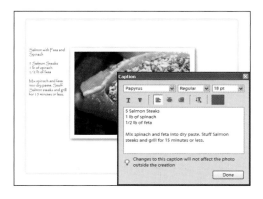

Project 12

Tools:

Photoshop Elements

Materials:

*Your photos or artwork
(optional)*

Create Your Own Custom Stationery

Create your own personal stationery using nothing but your imagination!

Custom stationery is just the answer when you need personal thank-you notes, family greetings, small club correspondence, or when you need a personalized gift for a special someone. In this project you will create stationery either using an existing photo or just starting from scratch.

1 **Open a new file.** Open Photoshop Elements 4.0. In the Welcome window, choose Edit and Enhance Photos. Once the program launches, choose File > New > Blank File. In the dialog that opens, select Letter from the Preset pop-up menu. If you are using a photograph, set the resolution to 300 for the best quality. The size of the photo should be fairly small so it won't be a problem even if you don't have a megapixel camera.

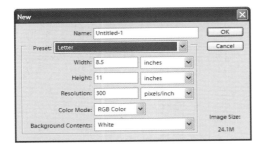

2 **Edit any artwork you want to use.** If you are going to be using your own artwork, you may have a few different types of files. For example, if you are creating something for a club you may have logo artwork in Adobe Illustrator, or you may be using a photo that is a .psd file.

If you are using a photograph, open it in Photoshop Elements and make any color corrections and other edits that the photo may need. Save a flattened version so that you can copy it directly into your stationery file.

③ Place your artwork. Place and size your artwork. Use one of the following techniques to place your artwork:

- In your artwork file, choose Select > All or press Ctrl+A. Then select Edit > Copy or press Ctrl+C. Return to your file and choose Edit > Paste, or press Ctrl+V.

- Alternately, choose File > Place. Navigate to your file and select Place.

After you place the artwork, use the Move tool ( ) to position it in the upper-left corner. If you are printing the stationery on a home printer, leave at least a quarter-inch margin from the edge of the document. This will ensure that your printer won't crop your artwork.

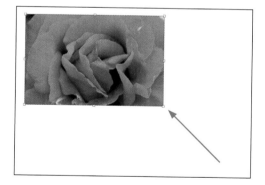

④ Pick a color for your border. Select the background layer and create a new layer by clicking the New Layer icon at the top of the Layers palette ( ). Click on the Set Foreground Color swatch in the toolbar to bring up the Color Picker. Select a color that will work with your photo or artwork. You may even want to use the eyedropper to pick up color from the art. Next, choose Edit > Fill Layer and choose a foreground color in the resulting dialog. This new color layer will be used for the border. Note: You can also use an adjustment layer.

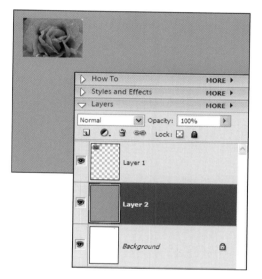

⑤ Add a border or accent shape. Select the Cookie Cutter tool (⬤) in the toolbar. Click the Shape icon on the options bar. In the Shapes palette, click the pop-up menu to select from all the different shapes libraries. Choose Frames.

Now, click and drag your border shape from the upper-left corner to the lower right. Press Enter to apply the shape. Ta-da! To add an accent shape instead of a frame, use the same steps, but instead of selecting Frames in the Shapes pop-up, select another library such as Ornaments, Flowers, or even Animals!

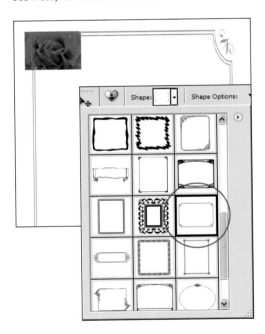

⑥ Add your text. We all will have different ideas of how much information we want on our stationery, but typically you will include at least your name, and often your address. Select the Text tool in the toolbar (**T**). Click in the area where you want your text to go and enter your text. (Use the Move tool for exact placement.)

⑦ Adjust your text. You may want to change the size and color of the text after you are finished. To do this, double-click the text layer to select it, and then use the options bar to change the font, size, and color.

8 **Save two versions of the final file.** As always, you want to save a version of your file with all the layers in case you want to change it. Save the layer version in a PSD format. Finally save a TIFF version for printing and leave the Layers option unchecked. Note: Instead of saving the file as a TIFF you could save as a PDF. This will give you a smaller file.

9 **Print and go!** Print multiple copies so that you'll have plenty of stationery for either handwritten notes or to pop in the printer for letters printed on the computer.

Tools:

Photoshop Elements
Cone Hat template

Materials:

Glossy paper

Create One-of-a-Kind Party Hats

Use this project to make your own party theme or as a fun party project!

With a little imagination, some scissors, tape, and elastic rubber bands, you can make your own party hats for whatever occasion you want. In this project, you will use the provided template along with fun styles in Photoshop Elements to create your one-of-a-kind party hat. As a variation, you can also use the Cookie Cutter tool to create crowns for the party host or hostess.

1 **Open the template.** Open Photoshop Elements 4.0. In the Welcome window, choose Edit and Enhance Photos. Once the program launches, choose File > Open. Navigate to the Project 13 folder and open the P13_tmp.psd file. Save the file with a new name.

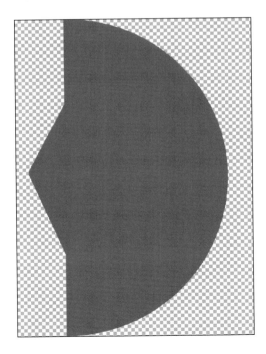

2 **Apply a pattern.** Select layer 0 in the Layers palette. Expand the Styles and Effects palette. Select Layer Styles and Patterns. Double-click on a pattern to apply it. If you don't like it, use the back button () to take it off.

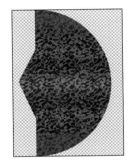
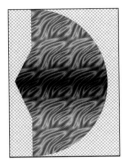
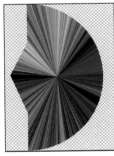

3 **Get creative!** At this point, the sky is the limit. You can add shapes using the Cookie Cutter tool (see Project 7), paint, or even start over with a new color.

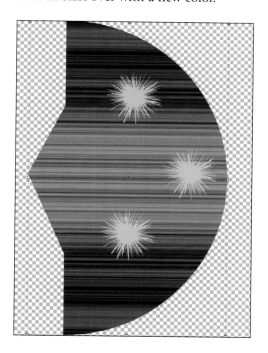

4 **Print and cut.** Save your file and print to glossy medium-weight paper. Once it's printed, simply cut out the shape and roll into a cone using either tape or staples to join the ends. Punch out holes in the side for your rubber band to hold the hat in place.

Variation: Create a crown using the Cookie Cutter tool

By now you may be familiar with Cookie Cutter tool. If you haven't used it yet, now is your chance! Just like the name implies, it cuts out a shape using the selected layer in the layers palette. This means that the layer can be a photo, pattern, or plain color- you decide. This variation shows you how to use the Cookie Cutter tool with a plain color but once you master that there is no limit to what you can use.

1 **Create a new file.** Choose File > New > Blank. Select 8x10 inches with at least 150-300 ppi for resolution.

2 **Fill your background layer with a color.** Double-click the background layer to convert it to a layer that can be edited. Click on the color swatch to bring up the Color Picker and select a color for your crown. Next, choose Edit > Fill Layer and select Foreground Color from the pop-up, then click OK.

3 **Pick your crown!** Select the Cookie Cutter tool. Click Shape on the options bar, then click the arrow to open the Shapes library. Choose Show All. Find your favorite crown, and drag the shape over your color layer. Press Enter to apply the shape.

Tools:

Photoshop Elements

Materials:

Your photos (optional)

Create Party Banners

Make your own custom party banner using photos, text and borders.

Have you ever wanted to personalize a party banner or maybe add a photo of the person being honored? In this project you will use the Cookie Cutter and Text tools to make your own personal party banner.

1 **Create your banner file.** Open Photoshop Elements. In the Welcome window, choose Edit and Enhance Photos. Once the program launches, choose File > New > Blank File. In the New dialog box, choose Custom under Preset to set your size. The resolution should be at least 250 to 300 ppi so if you are using any photos, you will want to check the size and resolution. Set your size in the Height and Width boxes.

2 **Add text.** Select the Text tool (**T**) and click anywhere in the file. Don't worry about the placement yet. Once you have typed your text, triple-click to select it all. At this point, you can change its font, size, and color.

To add more text, just click the Text tool anywhere on the file and a new text layer will be created.

HAPPY BIRTHDAY GEORGE!

3 **Move the text into position.** Click on the text layer in the Layers palette and select the Move tool (➤⊕). You will see the bounding box around your text layer within the window. Simply drag the text where you want it to go.

4 **Add any other artwork**. Now that you have the text where you want it, this is a good time to add any additional artwork. To bring in a photograph, simply open the photo in Photoshop Element and use the move tool to drag it into the banner file. Alternatively, you can copy and paste it into the banner file. Use the shortcut Ctrl+A to select the text, then Ctrl+C to copy it, and finally Ctrl+V to paste it into the banner. In this example, I have added some simple stars using the Cookie Cutter tool (⬤)which you will be using in the next step.

HAPPY BIRTHDAY GEORGE!
IT'S BEEN A WILD YEAR

5 **Create your banner layer.** Click the Adjustment Layer icon (⬤) located at the top of the Layers palette. Choose Solid Color from the pop-up and select a color from the resulting Color Picker. You will use this new layer to create your background banner shape.

HAPPY BIRTHDAY GEORGE!
IT'S BEEN A WILD YEAR

6 **Choose your banner!** Select the Cookie Cutter tool. Click Shape on the options bar, then click the arrow to open the Shapes library. Choose Banners, and select the one you want. Click outside the palette to close it. Now, click and drag the from the upper left to the lower right, and press Enter to apply the shape.

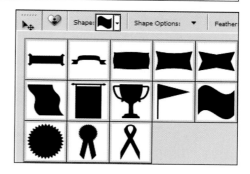

7 **Save as a PDF.** Since most banners are quite large, file size should be considered. Choose File > Save As and choose PDF as your file type, then select Save A Copy. Under Compression, choose High for the best quality.

Project 15

Tools:

Photoshop Elements

Materials:

Magnet sheet with sticky backing

Create Fun Magnets

Decorate your refrigerator with some new and functional artwork.

I don't know about your refrigerator door, but ours is virtual gallery of magnets, art, and household notes. In this project you can create all kinds of custom magnets, displaying such things as the date for an upcoming big event, a list of the members of your softball team, or even a business card. You name it! Best of all, you can use your own artwork or start from scratch. In the example piece, I have created a file with some text on a background that I want to finish up with some more decorations using the Cookie Cutter tool.

1 **Set the size of your magnet.** Open Photoshop Elements. In the Welcome window, choose Edit and Enhance Photos. Once the program launches, choose File > New > Blank File. In the dialog box that opens, select the Preset pop-up and choose your size. A typical size is 2x3 inches, which is slightly smaller than a business card. If you want a custom size, select Custom and set your height and width. The resolution should be at least 150 ppi. Save your new file and leave it open.

2 **Edit any artwork you want to use.** If you are going to be using your own artwork, you may have a few different types of files. For example, you may have logo artwork if you are creating something for a sports team, or you may be using your new baby's photograph for the grandparents. In either case, the resolution should match your magnets. Artwork that is vector based, such as an Adobe Illustrator file, can be resized inside the template.

If you are using a photograph, open it in Photoshop Elements and make any color corrections and other edits that the photo may need. Save a flattened version so that you copy it directly into your new magnet file.

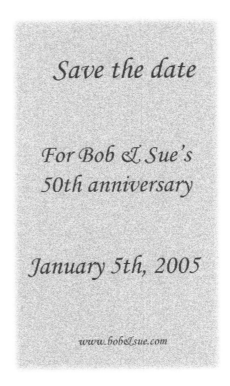

3 **Place your artwork**. Place and size your artwork. Use one of the following techniques to place your artwork:

- In your artwork file, choose Select > All or press Ctrl+A. Then select Edit > Copy (or press Ctrl+C), then go back to your magnet file and choose Edit > Paste (or press Ctrl+V).

- For vector artwork such as logos, begin by choosing File > Place. Navigate to your file and select Place. Use the handles to resize the image after it is placed in the template. After you place the artwork, use the Move tool (⊹) to position it.

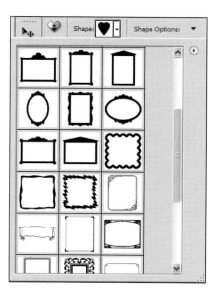

4 **Add a border shape.** Use the following steps to add a border using the Cookie Cutter tool:

- In your magnet file, select the Cookie Cutter tool (♥) in the toolbar. Click Shape in the options bar. In the Shapes palette, click the pop-up menu and select from the shapes libraries. Choose Frames. But wait; don't use that shape yet.

- Click the Adjustment Layer icon (⬤) located at the top of the Layers palette. Choose Solid Color from the pop-up and select a color from the resulting Color Picker. You will use this new layer to create your border.

- Now, click and drag your border shape from the upper left to the lower right. Press Enter to apply the shape. Ta-da!

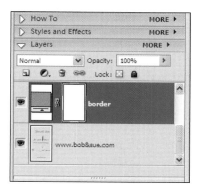

5 **Add other decorations using the Cookie Cutter tool.** Select another shape (not a Frame shape) to add some more decoration. Follow the same steps as you did to create the frame.

6 **Save two versions of the final file.** As always, you want to save a version of your file with all the layers in case you want to change it. Save the layer version in a .psd format. Finally, save a .tif version for printing and leave the Layers option unchecked.

7 **Print and go!** Depending on what your final artwork is, you may want to print a multiple layout. See Project 3 for more information on printing a multiple layout. When you have your final print, smooth it over your sticky-back magnet sheet and use an Exacto knife to cut it out.

Tools:

Photoshop Elements

Materials:

Your photos or artwork
Temporary tattoo film and
adhesive (available online)

Create Your Own Temporary Tattoos

Using your own inkjet printer you can make custom temporary tattoos.

Have you ever wanted to experience what it would be like to have a tattoo? Maybe you want to surprise your friends, or just have one for a party. While there are a lot of pre-fab ones you can buy at a store, the technology is available that allows you to create your own design and print it out at home. So, if you want to test a real tattoo out before committing, or just have one done for fun, this project is a great way to go.

1 **Open a new file.** Open Photoshop Elements 4.0. In the Welcome window, choose Edit and Enhance Photos. Once the program launches, choose File > New > Blank File. Set your width, height, and resolution to match that of your artwork. Ideally, your resolution should be around 300 ppi for the best quality. If you are planning to create your artwork in this file, set it to the size you want. Note: It's generally easier to work with smaller sizes (3x4, for example) than larger ones such as 8x10.

2 **Place any artwork you want to use.** If you are working with vector artwork from another program such as Illustrator, you can resize it without losing any quality. (To learn more about sizing your photos, see Project 2.) To place your artwork, choose File > Place. Navigate to your file on your hard drive, select it, and then click OK. Once it is placed in your document, you can move and resize your artwork if needed before you press the Enter key to accept it. Hold down the Shift key when resizing to keep the proper aspect ratio.

3 **Reverse your image.** Because your image will be transferred from the film to your body, it needs to be reversed to be seen correctly. This is especially important if you are including words. To reverse your image, choose Image > Rotate > Flip Layer Horizontal.

4 **Test on plain paper.** Before printing it to the temporary tattoo film, you want to test your image on regular plain paper. After you print it, make any adjustments to the color or brightness, and then print another test to make sure it is exactly how you want it.

5 **Print on the tattoo film**. Insert the film and print! After you print the image, use an Exacto knife to cut around it, leaving a border of about 1/16 of an inch. Each manufacturer will have its own set of guidelines on how to create the transfer from there. Read them carefully before proceeding.

Work with your printer

All printers are different; some are known for printing extra heavy on black, for instance. If you are having problems with this, you may want to examine your printer settings for any adjustments you can make.

Brighten it up

Flat colors can show imperfections in printing easily. To account for this, simply adjust the brightness in the artwork to make the ink less heavy.

Use gradients

To avoid the printing issues associated with flat colors, use gradients.

Tools:

Photoshop Elements

Materials:

*Photo-transfer paper
Your image and fabric
Templates*

Create Custom T-shirts

Use the project templates and photo-transfer paper to place photos, artwork, and text on T-shirts.

Have you wanted to create your own T-shirt design, maybe for a sports team or special event? This project gives you the templates for adding images, logos, and slogans to T-shirts and other items. All you need are your own images and ideas.

1 **Check the size of your artwork.** Depending on what you're creating, you may have a few different types of files. For example, if you are creating something for a sports team, you may have logo artwork, or you may be using your new baby's photograph on a tote bag for grandma.

In either case, the logo or image dimensions need to be approximately 6 x 9 inches with a resolution of 150 pixels per inch. The exact dimensions will vary depending on the template you use, so look at the template size first. To check the resolution and size of your image in Photoshop Elements, choose Image > Resize > Image Size. For more information see "Use the correct image size" in Project 2.

Artwork that is vector based, such as an Adobe Illustrator file, can be resized inside the template.

2 **Edit your photograph.** Open the photograph that you want to use in Photoshop Elements. Make any color corrections and other edits that the photo may need.

3 **Save two versions.** After you have finished making edits to your image, choose File > Save As. Rename the file and save it in a Photoshop format. This will save any layers in the file in case you want to make changes later.

Next, choose File > Save As and select TIFF as the format, being sure to deselect the Layers option box.

Save the file with the .tif extension so you don't replace the working version. Close the file.

4 **Edit the template.** In the Project 17 folder on the companion site, open the template that you want to use in Photoshop Elements and save it with a new name. Notice that there is a text layer for a slogan or company saying on the Layers palette.

Double-click the text layer to select the text. Enter your own message or company slogan. Change the font and size using the pop-up menus on the Type options bar. To change the color of the text, click the color swatch on the Type options bar. Select a new color using the Color Picker that appears; then click OK. You can also change the arc or bend of the text by selecting the text and then clicking the Warp Text tool located on the options bar.

P17a_tmp.psd

P17b_tmp.psd

P17c_tmp.psd

P17d_tmp.psd

P17e_tmp.psd

P17f_tmp.psd

5 **Place and size your artwork.** Use one of the following techniques to place your artwork.

If you are using a template with a shape for your image be sure to select the Place Image Here layer. This is an important step because it ensures that your image is positioned below the layer mask. If there is a layer in the template you do not wish to use, click on the eye next to the layer to turn it off.

• Choose Select > All or press Ctrl+A. Then select Edit > Copy or press Ctrl+C. Return to your template file, and choose Edit > Paste or press Ctrl+V.

• Or choose File > Place. Navigate to your file and select Place. Use the handles to resize the image after it is placed in the template. After you place the artwork, use the Move tool to position it.

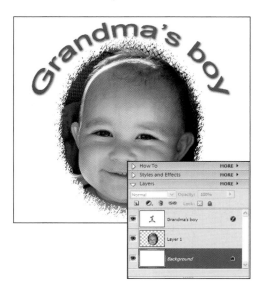

6 **Save and print your file.** Repeat step 3 and save two versions of the new file: one Photoshop version and one TIFF version for printing. After saving the file, choose File > Print to print your file on photo-transfer paper. Note: Different manufacturers of photo-transfer papers have different printing setup requirements. Follow the manufacturer's instructions.

Printing a mirror image

Read the detailed instructions that come with the photo-transfer paper. Most papers work from a mirror image so that the image and text will be correct when ironed onto a fabric. If your printer does not have a mirror or reverse setting, use the following steps to create a mirror image:

1 In your TIFF file, choose Image > Rotate > Flip Horizontal.

2 Choose File > Print and print according to the instructions of the paper manufacturer.

Prepping the fabric

○ Prewash the material to remove any residual chemicals.

○ Rinse clean with no softeners or additives.

Ironing

○ Preheat the iron using the highest setting and drain any water from steam irons.

○ A normal ironing board is too soft so use a low, hard surface such as a counter or table at waist or knee level. This allows you to lean over the iron and exert strong pressure along with the high heat. DO NOT USE A GLASS TABLE!

○ Place a wrinkle-free pillowcase on the ironing surface. Center the transfer area of your fabric over the pillowcase.

Project 18

Tools:

Photoshop Elements

Materials:

Your photo

Blend Multiple Images to Create Artistic Collages

Make striking imagery by blending multiple photos.

Have you ever seen a collage of images that, pieced together, meant more than each image separately? Such a grouping is often used to tell a story or to make a visual connection for the viewer.

In this project, you will learn how to blend separate images together to create one illustration. Then, if you want, you can add text and graphics.

1 **Get started.** Open the images you plan to blend together. Make any edits you desire to each image, such as correcting color or lighting.

2 **Size your images.** The image size and resolution should be approximately the same for both images for a good blend. For example, if your final result is to be a 8x10-inch print, then both images should be 8x10 and 250 to 300 dpi. If one is smaller or at a lower resolution, it may be too small. A larger image can always be sampled down, but if you try and resample an image to make it larger, the quality suffers. For tips on image resizing and resolution, see "Use the correct image size" in Project 2.

3 **Extract your image using the new Magic Extract tool.** Click the image you want in the foreground of your illustration and choose Image > Magic Extractor. This is a really great new feature that will allow you to extract the part of the image you want with virtually no effort.

In the Magic Extractor dialog box, follow the steps to get the best extraction. Don't worry if there is a little rough edge left on your image; you will take care of that later.

As always, you should have a backup of the original file. Save the new extracted version with a new name. This will ensure that you have an original copy to go back to if needed.

4 **Copy the new image into your background.** Copy the new extracted image: First press Ctrl+A to select everything in your image, and then press Ctrl+C to copy it. Click on your background image in the Photo Bin to open it. Paste your image into the background image by using the shortcut Ctrl+V.

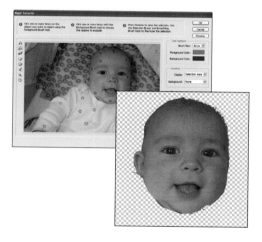

5 **Blend the two images.** Place your cursor over the extracted layer in the Layers palette. Hold down the Ctrl key and click in the layer. Notice that it is now selected in the window. Choose Select > Modify > Border. The resulting dialog box lets you smooth the edges to blend in with the background. You will want this border selection to be substantial. For this image, which is 8x10 inches at 300-pixel dpi, the border selection is set to 40. Once you set the size, click OK. Next, choose Filter > Blur > Gaussian Blur. Adjust the blur to a size you like using the preview as a guide. Save your working file in Photoshop format (.psd) so you have a version with all the layers.

Variation: Change modes

Add other graphics. Experiment with adding graphics from programs such as Adobe Illustrator or creating them in Photoshop Elements. Try the different blend modes to see what type of effect you get.

Blending images can be a tricky process. Often, it's good to work with one image that creates more of a pattern and one that is the focal point.

OPPOSITES DO ATTRACT! When blending images, it often works well to have one of the images have more of a texture or to be more abstract than the other.

Project 19

Tools:

Photoshop Elements

Materials:

Your photos
Music file or computer mic
for recording narration

Create a Slide Show with Sound

Now you can share your vacation images with friends and family everywhere by creating a slideshow using the Slideshow feature of Photoshop Elements.

The Slideshow feature is terrific for creating a personal slideshow to run on your desktop PC, to post online, or burn to DVD to play on your television. Plus, using the new audio feature, you can add sound to your slideshow, providing narration or some ambient music.

1 **Organize your images.** Open the Photo Browser and make the necessary edits to the images you plan to use in the slideshow. The slideshow will be shown full screen, so for the best image quality the size should be at least 1280x1024 pixels with a resolution of 72 ppi. (See "Use the correct image size" in Project 2.)

2 **Choose the slideshow images.** After you have edited the images, put them into a collection in the Organizer. (For help creating your collection, see project 1.) Double-click your new collection to open it. After you open your collection, you will see only those images, and they will automatically be selected for your slideshow. At this point, you can drag the images into a different viewing order, and that order will be retained for the slideshow.

3 **Set up your slideshow options.** Click the Create button (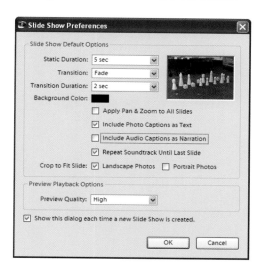) and select the first option, Slide Show. In the next dialog box, specify how long you want each slide to last, the transition type, and the duration. The default setting for advancing the images is 5 seconds. Decide what time works best for your slides and enter that value. Next, choose the transition that you want to occur between slides. You may want to experiment to see which you like best. You can leave the rest of the settings at their defaults and click Next.

4 **Add a title slide.** In the Edit Slide Show window, there are a wide variety of things you can do. Everything from reordering your images (if you didn't order them in the collection), to adding graphics, text, sound, or even adding other images you may have forgotten. You are going to create a title slide.

First, click the Add Blank Slide button. Change the color by clicking on the color swatch in the Properties palette. Click the Add Text button in the toolbar. Type your title text in the dialog box. Click OK when you are done. You can change the font, color, and size in the Properties palette. For a final touch, click the Graphics button in the Extras palette to access frames. To add a frame, double-click on it in the palette. When you have your title slide looking the way you want, drag it to the beginning in the slide sort at the bottom of the window.

5 **Add your audio.** This next step has two different sets of directions, depending on what type of audio you are going to add to your show.

If you want to add an audio file, such as background music, then click on the bottom of the Slide Sorter on the link Click Here to Add Audio to Your Slide Show. Navigate to your audio file, select it, and click Open.

If you are going to add narration to your slides, then click the Narration button in the Extras palette. Select the slide you want to add narration to in the Slide Sorter and use the recording controls to record your narration. Once you stop recording, you will see a microphone icon on the slide. Click the Preview button to see what your final slideshow will look like.

6 **Save your slideshow.** We've arrived at the moment you have been waiting for! Click the Output button. You have a number of options: Save as file, Burn to Disc, Email, or Send to TV. If you are uncertain which is best for you, click on the option to see helpful hints. Choose the one that suits your needs, and click OK. Follow the steps for your selection and you're done!

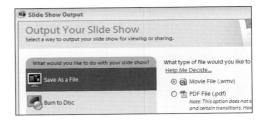

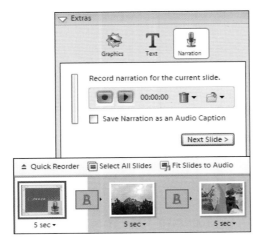

Project 20

Create a Web Photo Gallery

Using nothing but your photographs and Photoshop Elements, you can create a sophisticated online gallery.

If you want to quickly post a gallery of images online, the Web Photo Gallery is just the thing. Photoshop Elements will create all of the HTML files as well as size and compress your images for the Web.

1 **Organize your image files.** First make the necessary edits to the images you will be posting to the Web. Photoshop Elements will resize the images and compress a copy of them for the Web. To be sure they are not accidentally compressed twice, save the files in a PSD format. After you are done editing the images, add them to the Organizer if you have not already done so.

2 **Select your gallery images and create a collection.** In the Organizer, select the images you want to use for your photo gallery and create a collection. (For more information on creating collections, see project 1.) Double-click the collection to view only those images. This will select them for your gallery. Drag the images in the order that you want them to appear in the gallery.

3 **Select your gallery style.** With your collection open, click the Create button. Under Creation Setup click HTML Photo Gallery, and then click OK. Under Adobe Web Photo Gallery you will see a thumbnail of all the images in your collection.

Use the Gallery Style pop-up menu to select how you want your images to appear. You will see a preview of the layout underneath. Note: Some of the Gallery styles also allow you to change the colors of the background and text.

4 **Create your title banner.** Click in the Title box of the Banner tab and enter your title. Enter any other information such as a subtitle or e-mail address. If you have any caption associated with your images, you can also select your font and font size here.

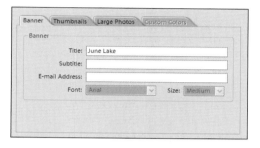

5 **Set your image sizes.** Click on the Large Photos and Thumbnails tabs to set the sizes for your final gallery images.

Make sure that the Resize Photos check box is selected. On the pop-up menu next to it, you can choose Large, Medium, Small, or Custom. Select the size that you want, then set your image quality. Remember, the higher the quality, the larger the file and the slower the download.

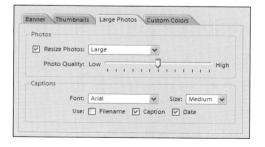

6 **Choose your destination**. Click the Browse button in the Destination box. Navigate to where you want your Web gallery folder to be saved.

Click Save and you're done! At this point you can preview your gallery in any Web browser before posting it to the Web.

Project 21

Tools:

Photoshop Elements

Materials:

Your photo

Create a Large, Mono-Color Background

Use a photo or illustration to make a large, mono-color background from brochures to Web pages.

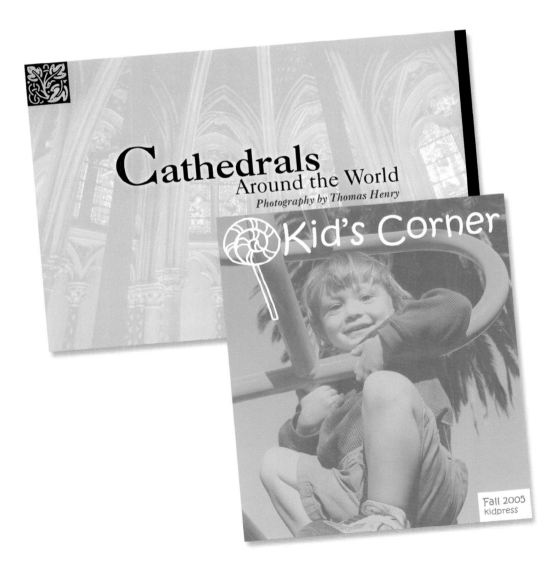

If you want to add an interesting background to the cover of a brochure or a Web page, you'll find this technique works great. Using a full-color image to fill an entire background normally requires a four-color process, which is costly, and for Web pages it typically results in a file that's too large for Web viewing. Another reason for creating a mono-color background is that you may want a subtle image; you want to add texture and content for your headline but nothing more. Whatever your reasons, in this project you will create a monochromatic background that will work for you.

1 Get started. Open your color photo in Photoshop Elements and resize it as necessary. Note: Generally, for an image to fill the entire background of a Web page, it should be 600 to 800 pixels wide and at least 480 pixels high. The image size you choose should be based on the amount of material on the page.

For information on resizing images, see "Use the correct image size" in project 2.

2 Convert a copy of your background layer to black and white. If your Layers palette is not open, click the Layers arrow in the palette bin. Select your background layer and drag it over the Create a New Layer icon (⬛) located at the top of the Layers palette. With your new layer selected, choose Enhance > Adjust Color > Remove Color.

3 Create a new color layer. You will use this color layer to colorize your black-and-white background. Click the Create Adjustment Layer icon (⬤) at the top of the Layers palette, then choose Solid Color from the pop-up menu. Choose a color using the Color Picker dialog box that appears. Remember that this is your primary background color, so select a color that will complement the rest of your artwork. After you select your new color, click OK. With your new layer still selected, choose Screen from the Mode pop-up menu and click OK. You should be able to see your background through the new layer.

Note: The great thing about using an adjustment layer is that you can always go back and change it easily. If your color is not quite right, double-click on the color swatch in the layer. This will bring up the Color Picker dialog box, and you can adjust or change the color.

4 Adjust the color opacity. Select the new color layer on the Layers palette. Use the Opacity slider at the top of the palette to adjust the layer's opacity. This affects the intensity of the color and allows more of the grayscale image to show through.

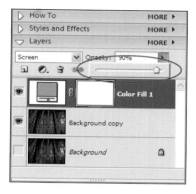

5 Save a working version of the file. Choose File > Save As and save the file in Photoshop format using a new name. This way, you will always have a version that contains all of your layers in case you want to make any changes.

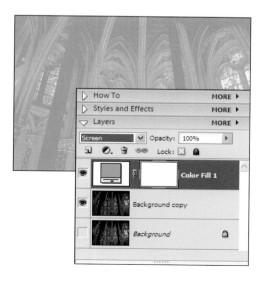

Variation: Optimize the image for the Web

After you have saved the working version, choose File > Save for Web. In the Save for Web dialog box, you will see two images. One is the original, and one is a preview of the optimized version. When you select different optimization settings, the changes will be reflected in this preview window.

Select JPEG from the Settings pop-up menu in the upper-right corner of the dialog box. Use the Quality slider to adjust the amount the image is compressed. The higher the quality of the image, the larger the file size. Since you are posting this image on the Web, you need to keep the file size small. With this in mind, start with a quality setting of 15. Check the file size underneath the image preview.

Try to keep the file size to around 20 to 40K or less. When you are happy with the quality and file size, click OK to save the Web version.

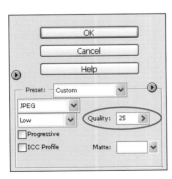

Adding outside graphic elements to your background image that complement the other graphics in your layout can make your final image more dynamic.

KEEP IT CLEAR

Don't allow the elements in the background to interfere with the page content.

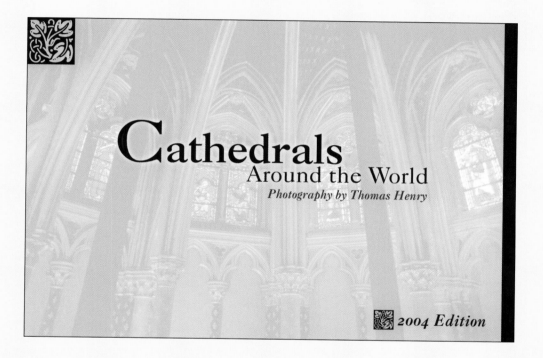

  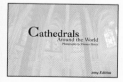 

A color that is too dark or saturated decreases the legibility of text and can be distracting.

A soft or more neutral background color helps show off the rest of your content.

Project 22

Tools:

Photoshop Elements

Materials:

*Your logo or artwork
(both optional)
Card stock paper
for printing*

Create Your Own Calling Card

*Making a name for yourself? This is a tried
and true starting point.*

Some people might call it a business card, but you don't have to have a business to have a card. You might just want a personal card that shows off your style and lets people know how to get in touch with you. Information can include your name, address, e-mail, and phone number. This project will walk you through creating a personalized calling card that you can print and cut out at home, or take to a service center.

1 **Open a new file.** Open Photoshop Elements 4.0. In the Welcome window, choose Edit and Enhance Photos. Once the program launches, choose File > New > Blank File. Choose inches from the Width pop-up menu and enter 3.5, then enter 2 under Height. Set your resolution to 300 for the highest quality.

2 **Place any artwork you want to use.** Because of the small size of a calling card, it is best to use simple imagery with few colors, such as line drawings or logos. If you do use a photo, try to make sure it is a close-up or headshot. To place your artwork, choose File > Place. Navigate to your file on your hard drive, select it, and then click OK. Once it is placed in your document, you can move and resize the photo before pressing the Enter key to accept it. Hold the Shift key down when resizing to keep the proper aspect ratio.

Alternatively, see Step 5 for adding an accent shape using the Cookie Cutter tool.

3 **Add your text.** You will probably want to include at least your name, address, phone number, and e-mail. Here you will create separate text blocks so that you can move them independently.

Select the Text tool in the toolbar (**T**). Click in the area where you want your first block of text to go and type your text. When you are done entering your text, move your cursor away from the text until you see the Move tool, then click. You can then click to create another separate text block. To move the separate text blocks, first select the text layer in the Layers palette, then use the Move tool (▶⊕) to move it into position.

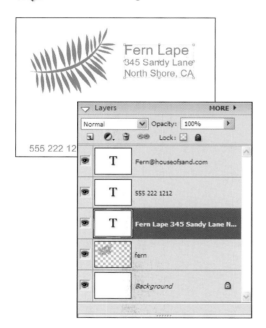

4 **Adjust your text.** You may want to change the size and color of the text after you are finished. To do this, double-click the text layer to select it, then use the options bar to change the font, size, and color.

5 **Add a border or accent shape.** Select the background layer and create a new layer by clicking the New Layer icon located at the top of the Layers palette (▣). Click on the Set Foreground Color swatch in the toolbar to bring up the Color Picker. Next, choose Edit > Fill Layer and choose a foreground color in the resulting dialog. (You can also click in the image area with the paint bucket tool (⬧) to achieve the same effect.) This new color layer will be used for the border.

Select the Cookie Cutter tool (♥) in the toolbar. Click the Shape icon on the options bar. In the Shapes palette, click the pop-up menu to select from all the different shapes libraries to choose a shape or frame that you want to use.

Now, click and drag your shape in the image area. To maintain the aspect ratio, hold the Shift key down while dragging. Press Enter to apply the shape.

6 **Save two versions of the final file.** As always, you want to save a version of your file with all the layers in case you want to change it. Save the layered version in a PSD format. Finally save a TIFF version for printing and leave the Layers option unchecked. Note: Instead of saving it as a TIFF, you can save it as a PDF. This will give you a smaller file.

7 **Set up your multiple-print layout.** If you are taking this to a service center, they will do this for you. If you are printing at home, you will want to set it up so that you are not wasting paper. With your file open, choose File > Print Multiple Photos. In the Print Photos dialog, choose Picture Package under Type of Print. Next, under Select a Layout, choose Letter (8) 2.5 x 3.5. Finally, select the check box Fill Page with First Photo. You will see your layout in the preview window.

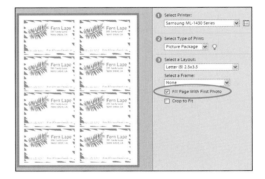

8 **Print and cut.** Insert your card stock paper and click Print in the Print dialog. For the cleanest cut, use an Exacto knife and a straight edge to cut out your cards.

Project 23

Tools:

Photoshop Elements

Materials:

Your photos
Read/write CDs
CD burner (either external
or internal)

Archive Your Images to a CD

Never lose your precious images again.
Back up your files to a CD in minutes.

So you've spent weeks organizing your images and days editing them and putting them into cards and other creations. The last thing you want is to lose anything! Or maybe you want to give a set of images to friends and family. This is perfect time to burn a CD. This project introduces you to Photoshop Elements' easy CD-burning feature.

1 **Select your images to back up.** This can be done in a few different ways. You can back up your whole Organizer, which could be quite large, or you can select the images you want to back up. To go the latter route, open the Organizer, select the first image you want to back up, and then while holding the Shift key, select the last image you want to back up. This will select all the images in between. To select multiple images that are in random order, use the Ctrl key instead. If you are backing up a collection, double-click the collection to open it and press Ctrl+A to select all of your images.

2 **Ready, set, go!** Select File > Burn. Select Copy/Move Files. This will allow you to copy just the selected images to a CD (or even a DVD) for either a personal backup or to share with friend. Click Next to go to the next step.

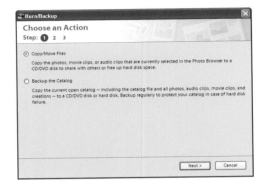

3 **Set your final option.** The step allows you to decide if you want to delete the files from your hard drive once you have burned them onto a CD. Photoshop Elements will create a small thumbnail for preview purposes. If you select the file for editing, you will be asked for the CD. Decide which direction you want go, and click Next.

4 **Burn that disk!** In the next dialog you will be asked to insert your disc. You will need to do this before going any further. Insert your disc and wait for Photoshop Elements to determine the write speed time estimates. Once it has determined the speed and time, enter the name for your CD and click Done. That's it!

Tools:

Photoshop Elements

Materials:

Your photos

Create a Contact Sheet for Your Image CD

Easily create thumbnails of all your images for a contact sheet that will fit into any jewel case.

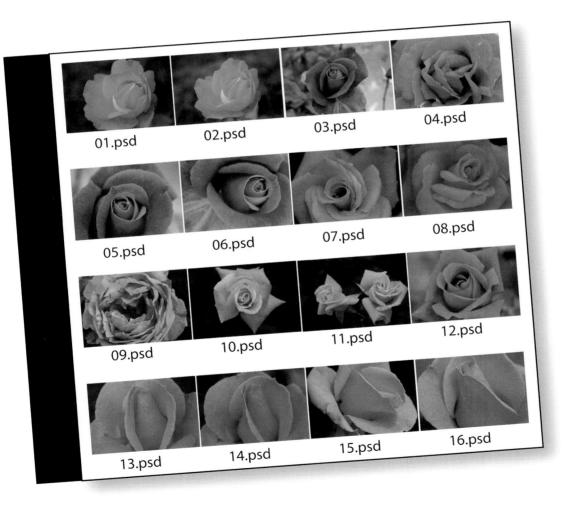

How often have you burned a CD of all your images but then wanted a quick way to reference them at a glance? Here's how to automatically set up a contact sheet in Photoshop Elements and send it to your printer.

1 **Get started.** Open the Organizer in Photoshop Elements and create a collection of the images you want on your contact sheet. (For more information on creating a collection, see Project 1.) Double-click your collection so that you are viewing only those images. Use the shortcut Ctrl+A to select all the images in your collection.

Alternatively, you can Shift-click the images in the Browser window to select the ones you want. This might work well if you don't have a lot of images.

2 **Preview your images.** Choose File > Print. All of your images will appear in the preview pane on the left side of the Print Selected Photos dialog box.

③ Set your print size. Click Page Setup and choose Printer, then Properties. Under Paper Size, choose Custom Paper and set the size to 4.75 for both Width and Height. Even if your paper is not this exact size, it's important to use these settings so that Photoshop Elements will know what margins to use for the contact sheet. When you are finished, click OK.

④ Select the layout. Under step 2 in the Print Selected Photos dialog box, click the Select Type of Print pop-up menu and choose Contact Sheet.

At this point you will want to set up any other options for your contact sheet, such as date, captions, and page numbers.

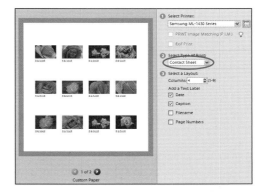

⑤ You're done! Click Print and you're ready to go!

Tools:

Photoshop Elements

Materials:

Your photos
Blank CD or DVD
Sticky-back labels

Create Custom CD or DVD Labels

Create your own CD labels for family photos, music mixes, or business use.

How often have you happened upon a mystery CD floating around your house with no explanation? Now, by creating a label that goes directly on the CD you can avoid that problem. Use this project to create fun, imaginative labels that will tell you exactly what is on a CD (or DVD) in one easy glance.

1 **Open a new file.** Open Photoshop Elements 4.0. In the Welcome window, choose Edit and Enhance Photos. Once the program launches, choose File > New > Blank File. Choose inches from the Width pop-up menu and enter 4.5, then enter 4.5 under Height. Set your resolution to 300 ppi for the highest quality.

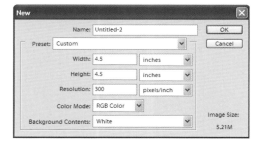

2 **Place any artwork you want to use.** Ideally, your photo should be approximately the same size and resolution as the label size. (To find out more about sizing your photos, see Project 2.) To place your artwork, choose File > Place. Navigate to your file on your hard drive, select it, and then click OK. Once it is placed in your document, you can move and resize; then press the Enter key to accept it. Be sure to hold the Shift key down when resizing to keep the proper aspect ratio.

3 **Crop your image to a CD.** Now, you want to crop your image to the label circle size. Select the Elliptical Marquee tool (○). Holding the Shift key down to constrain the proportion, click and drag from the upper-left corner to the lower-right corner. You should be able to see the selection marquee circling your image. Next, choose Select > Inverse from the menu bar. Press the Delete or Backspace key to delete the edges.

4 **Create a core area.** The core area of the CD is the 1.5-inch circle inside the CD or DVD. You will clear this space using the Elliptical Marquee tool again. First, choose View > Rulers. (Note: You can also choose to View Grid at the same time if you want.) If the Info palette is not already open, choose Window > Info.

With the Elliptical Marquee tool selected, set the Mode to Fixed Aspect Ratio, and set both Width and Height to 1. Set your cursor at 2.25 inches down and 2.25 inches across. Holding down the Alt key to select out from the center point, click and drag until you see 1.5 inches for Width and Height on the Info palette. Press the Delete or Backspace key to delete the area.

5 **Add your title text.** Select the Text tool in the toolbar (**T**). Click in the area where you want your title text to go and type your text. When you've finished, move your cursor away from the text until you see the Move tool (⬛⊕), then click. If you want, you can then click to create another separate text block. To move the separate text blocks, first select the text layer in the Layers palette, and then use the Move tool to move it into position

6 **Adjust your text.** You may want to change the size and color of the text after you have finished. To do this, double-click the text layer to select it, then use the options bar to change the font, size, and color.

7 **Save two versions of the final file.** As always, you want to save a version of you file with all the layers in case you want to change it. Save the layered version in a PSD format. Finally, save a TIFF version for printing and leave the Layers option deselected. Note: Instead of saving it as a TIFF, you can save it as a PDF, which will give you a smaller file.

8 **Print.** Check with your CD labels for any directions for how to position the image for printing. To position the image, choose File > Print > Deselect Center Image. You can then enter your own margins for printing.

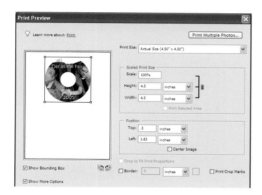

Index

Fixed Aspect Ratio, 121

flattened versions, 30

Flip Layer Horizontal command, 79

frames. *See* borders

G

galleries

creating, 97–100

image size for, 99

saving, 100

selecting images for, 98

style of, 99

title banner for, 99

Gaussian Blur command, 30, 90

Get Photos command, 2

gradients, 80

Grayscale mode, 6, 43

H

Healing Brush tool, 9–10

highlights, 26

Hue slider, 44

I

Image menu

Enhance, 31

Magic Extractor, 89

Mode, 6, 22, 43

Resize, 6, 42

Rotate, 8, 79, 85

Image Size command, 6

images. *See* photos

Include in Organizer check box, 56

InDesign, 42, 45

Index color mode, 6

Info palette, 121

Inverse command, 29, 121

J

JPEG format, 104

L

labels

creating, 119–123

images for, 120–121

printing, 123

saving, 122

text for, 122

Layer Via Copy command, 30

layers

adjustment, 36, 44, 71, 75, 103

Background, 30, 32, 38

blending modes for, 23

creating new, 22, 30

naming, 22

lighting, correcting, 10

M

Magic Eraser tool, 24

Magic Extract tool, 89

Magic Selection Brush tool, 28

magnets

artwork for, 74–75

borders for, 75

creating, 73–76

printing, 76

saving, 76

size of, 74

Mask mode, 28, 33

masking, 28–29, 33

mirror images, 85

mistakes, correcting, 24

modes, 6, 22

mono-color backgrounds, 101–105

Move tool, 32, 61, 62, 70, 75, 109, 122

N

New Collection command, 2

New Layer icon, 22, 61, 109

New Sub-Category command, 4

New Tag command, 4

newsletters, publishing photos in, 41–45

O

online photo galleries

creating, 97–100

image size for, 99

saving, 100

selecting images for, 98

style of, 99

title banner for, 99

Opacity slider, 103

Open command, 66

Organizer

backing up, 112

benefits of, 2

creating collections in, 1–3

creating tags in, 4

selecting multiple images in, 15, 18, 112, 116

P

paint bucket tool, 109

Paintbrush tool, 23

panoramic images, 17–20

party banners

artwork for, 71

creating, 69–71

file size of, 71

printing, 71

style of, 71

text for, 70

party hats

creating, 65–68

patterns for, 66

printing, 67

Paste command, 61

patterns, 66

stationery

   accent shapes for, 62

   artwork for, 60–61

   borders for, 61–62

   creating, 59–63

   printing, 63

   saving, 63

   text for, 62

Step Backward command, 30

Straighten and Crop Image command, 8

Styles and Effects palette, 26, 31, 66

T

T-shirts

   artwork for, 82, 84

   creating, 81–85

   mirror images for, 85

   printing, 84–85

   text for, 83

tags, 4

tattoos, temporary

   artwork for, 78

   creating, 77–80

   printing, 79–80

   reversing image for, 79

Text tool, 62, 70, 109, 122

thank-you notes, 60

TIFF format, 43, 63, 110, 122

Type options bar, 83

U

undo, 24

Unsharp Mask filter, 11, 43

V

Vanishing Point tool, 19

View menu, 121

W

Warp Text tool, 83

Web page backgrounds, 101–105

Web photo galleries

   creating, 97–100

   image size for, 99

   saving, 100

   selecting images for, 98

   style of, 99

   title banner for, 99

Window menu

   Cascade, 32

   Color Swatches, 23

   Info, 121

   Layers, 22

Z

Zoom tool, 11, 28